NEW EVE

30 DEVOTIONS FOR OLDER PEOPLE BY RITA MCLAUGHLAN

God's Compassionate Heart

Other *New Every Day* titles

God's Great Faithfulness

God's Eternal Gifts

God's Unfailing Love

Published 2012 by CWR, Waverley Abbey House, Waverley Lane, Farnham, Surrey GU9 8EP, UK. Registered Charity No. 294387. Registered Limited Company No. 1990308.

For list of National Distributors visit www.cwr.org.uk/distributors
Song lyrics on Day 12 from 'Tell out, my soul' by Timothy Dudley-Smith (b. 1926), © Timothy Dudley-Smith in Europe and Africa, © Hope Publishing Company in the United States of America and the rest of the world. Last verse reproduced by permission of Oxford University Press. All rights reserved.
Unless otherwise indicated, all Scripture references are from the Holy Bible: New International Version (NIV), copyright © 1973, 1978, 1984 by the International Bible Society.
Other Scripture versions used:
GNB: Good News Bible © 1996, 1971, 1976 American Bible Society
NLT: Holy Bible New Living Translation, © 1996. Used by permission of Tyndale House Publishers Inc.
Concept development, editing, design and production by CWR
Cover image: istock/chinaface
Printed in the UK by Linney Print
ISBN: 978-1-85345-853-8

Solomon asks for wisdom

*S*olomon answered, '... O LORD God, fulfil the promise you made to my father. You have made me king over a people who are so many that they cannot be counted, so give me the wisdom and knowledge I need to rule over them. Otherwise, how would I ever be able to rule this great people of yours?' God replied to Solomon, 'You have made the right choice. Instead of asking for wealth or treasure or fame or the death of your enemies or even for long life for yourself, you have asked for wisdom and knowledge so that you can rule my people, over whom I have made you king. I will give you wisdom and knowledge. And in addition, I will give you more wealth, treasure, and fame than any king has ever had before or will ever have again.' *2 Chronicles 1:8–12 (GNB)*

The young king chose well when he asked God to give him wisdom. He needed it in his role as ruler over Israel. But we all need wisdom in our lives, whether we are rich and famous or just ordinary people. We need to know how to live prudently, how to relate to others, how to make plans for the future, how to help others ...

There is a difference between knowledge and wisdom – the first is about gathering facts, the second about applying those facts to daily living.

Prayer:
Thank You, Father, for King Solomon's writings. Please help me to learn from them this week. Amen.

Solomon shares his wisdom

*T*he proverbs of Solomon, son of David and king of Israel. Here are proverbs that will help you to recognize wisdom and good advice, and understand sayings with deep meaning. They can teach you how to live intelligently and how to be honest, just, and fair. They can make an inexperienced person clever and teach young people how to be resourceful. These proverbs can even add to the knowledge of the wise and give guidance to the educated, so that they can understand the hidden meanings of proverbs and the problems that the wise raise. *Proverbs 1:1–6 (GNB)*

Solomon wrote these wise sayings thousands of years ago but they are just as relevant today as they were then, covering almost every aspect of life.

There is so much in the book of Proverbs that we cannot cover it all in these notes but I would recommend that, if you have a Bible, you find Proverbs and dip into it for yourself, just a little at a time. You will be richly rewarded. There is practical advice for the young and the old, reminders about the best way to act, how to relate to others, how to conduct your life and, above all, the benefits of wisdom.

Prayer:
Lord God, I want to be wise in the way that I live, to please You in all aspects of my life. Amen.

The value of wisdom

*W*isdom is more valuable than jewels; nothing you could want can compare with it. Wisdom offers you long life, as well as wealth and honour. Wisdom can make your life pleasant and lead you safely through it. Those who become wise are happy; wisdom will give them life. Hold on to your wisdom and insight, my son. Never let them get away from you ... You can go safely on your way and never even stumble. You will not be afraid when you go to bed, and you will sleep soundly through the night. *Proverbs 3:15–18,21–24 (GNB)*

The words 'wisdom and insight' (v.21), are translated in some other versions of the Bible as 'sound judgment and discernment' (eg NIV). The writer is implying that we should give time to consider before making decisions, not throwing caution to the winds and making the mistake of being too hasty. Many a wrong move has been made by people who speak or act too quickly without thinking about all the implications of the matter. 'Hold on to wisdom,' Solomon advises. 'Don't let it get away in the heat of the moment.' Sound advice! And the benefits include the ability to sleep soundly at night – how practical is that?

Prayer:
Father God, I ask You today to remind me, when I have decisions to make, to take time to consider and to act and speak with wisdom at all times. Amen.

Listen to good advice

*S*ensible people accept good advice. People who talk foolishly will come to ruin ... People who listen when they are corrected will live, but those who will not admit that they are wrong are in danger ... Stupid people always think they are right. Wise people listen to advice ... Arrogance causes nothing but trouble. It is wiser to ask for advice ... Conceited people do not like to be corrected; they never ask for advice from those who are wiser ... If you listen to advice and are willing to learn, one day you will be wise.
Proverbs 10:8,17; 12:15; 13:10; 15:12; 19:20 (GNB)

We, of the older generation, do not always like listening to advice. We have the experience. Haven't we been through all this before? Don't we know better than the young? But however old we are, however much we have been through, there is always more to learn if we are humble enough to listen. Wise people are always willing to accept correction and advice, even from younger folk. And how proud our grandchildren are if they can tell us something we didn't know!

Conceited people are hard to live with – much better to be humble and willing to learn.

To think about:
Am I a good listener when younger folk want to give me advice?

Think before you speak

A wise, mature person is known for his understanding. The more pleasant his words, the more persuasive he is.

Intelligent people think before they speak; what they say is then more persuasive. Kind words are like honey – sweet to the taste and good for your health.

People with a hot temper do foolish things; wiser people remain calm.

A gentle answer quietens anger, but a harsh one stirs it up. When wise people speak they make knowledge attractive, but stupid people spout nonsense.
Proverbs 16:21,23–24; 14:17; 15:1–2 (GNB)

Yesterday we thought about listening. Solomon also had wise words on the subject of speech. Two thoughts come out plainly in this passage – that we should think before we speak and that our words should always be pleasant. We all need wisdom at times, to know how to answer argumentative or crotchety people, for example. Kind, gentle words often defuse a situation and lead to a positive conversation rather than further argument. We should seek to be encouraging, kind and gentle in our speech.

Prayer:
Please help me, Lord, to consider what I say, to use words wisely and always to be pleasant when talking. Amen

Be generous

*S*ome people spend their money freely and still grow richer. Others are cautious, and yet grow poorer. Be generous, and you will be prosperous. Help others, and you will be helped. People curse someone who hoards grain, waiting for a higher price, but they praise the one who puts it up for sale. If your goals are good, you will be respected, but if you are looking for trouble, that is what you will get. Those who depend on their wealth will fall like the leaves of autumn, but the righteous will prosper like the leaves of summer.

Be generous and share your food with the poor. You will be blessed for it. *Proverbs 11:24–28; 22:9 (GNB)*

In the present economic situation many people are feeling the pinch and finding it difficult to cope financially. Older folk particularly find increasing fuel bills hard to pay. God does not expect us to neglect our own well-being in order to help others but He does ask us to give generously when we can.

There are other ways to help besides giving money – invite a lonely person in for a cup of tea, comfort a friend suffering bereavement, take a meal to someone who is housebound. We can be generous with our time as well as our money.

Prayer:
Dear generous God, please help me to share what You have given me. Amen.

Stay cheerful and at peace

*B*eing cheerful keeps you healthy. It is a slow death to be gloomy all the time. *Proverbs 17:22 (GNB)*

A cheerful heart is good medicine, but a crushed spirit dries up the bones. *Proverbs 17:22*

Smiling faces make you happy, and good news makes you feel better. *Proverbs 15:30 (GNB)*

A heart at peace gives life to the body, but envy rots the bones. *Proverbs 14:30*

Solomon was wise before his time. Modern medicine has discovered that a cheerful, positive attitude towards life goes a long way towards encouraging both mental and physical health. We who believe in God and place our reliance on Him have every reason to be cheerful and at peace, knowing that He takes care of us in all situations. A smile costs nothing and is infectious – we can encourage others daily just by our general demeanour and if this gives an opportunity to spread the good news about Jesus, that is an added bonus. Cheerfulness is a double blessing – good for ourselves and for those around us.

For action:
'... if any of you lacks wisdom, he should pray to God, who will give it to him; because God gives generously and graciously to all. But when you pray, you must believe and not doubt at all.' James 1:5–6 (GNB)

God's love

God is love

*D*ear friends, let us love one another, for love comes from God. Everyone who loves has been born of God and knows God. Whoever does not love does not know God, because God is love. This is how God showed his love among us: He sent his one and only Son into the world that we might live through him. This is love: not that we loved God, but that he loved us and sent his Son as an atoning sacrifice for our sins. *1 John 4:7–10*

This week we are going to think about God's love, what it is like and what it means for us. In this passage John tells us that God *is* love. His very nature is love and He can never be anything but loving.

Even when He has to discipline us He does it in love, for our good. And because He loves us so much He sent His Son, Jesus, into the world to show us what love really is. Jesus gave His life for us on the cross as a sacrifice for our sins, yours and mine, so that we may be forgiven and come into the presence of the Father Himself. He wants you to know Him, to experience His love every day.

Prayer:
Thank You, Father, that You love me so much.
I trust in You and receive Your love today. Amen.

God loved so He gave ...

For God so loved the world that he gave his one and only Son, that whoever believes in him shall not perish but have eternal life. For God did not send his Son into the world to condemn the world, but to save the world through him. Whoever believes in him is not condemned, but whoever does not believe stands condemned already because he has not believed in the name of God's one and only Son. *John 3:16–18*

God loved this sinful world so much that He sent His Son, Jesus, into the world, not to condemn us but to save us from our sins by giving His life for us on the cross of Calvary. Have you ever thought what it must have cost our heavenly Father to see His Son suffering rejection, insults and unimaginable pain as He died? Yet such was God's love for us, for you and me, that both the Father and the Son were prepared to make that sacrifice so that we might be forgiven and receive eternal life – to know His presence with us now and live with Him forever.

To think about:
'... God demonstrates His own love for us in this: While we were still sinners, Christ died for us'.
Romans 5:8
God did not wait until we were good; in His love He reached down to us in our sinfulness.

The earth filled with God's love

*F*or the word of the LORD is right and true; he is faithful in all he does. The LORD loves righteousness and justice; the earth is full of his unfailing love. *Psalm 33:4–5*

The earth is filled with your love, O LORD; teach me your decrees. *Psalm 119:64*

The Bible tells us that the earth is filled with God's love. There is nowhere you can go that God's love cannot reach. In a busy city or out in a desert, in the midst of your family or on your own, in church or a crowded supermarket, that place is full of God's unfailing love. But many people ask: if God loves this world so much, why is there so much suffering? Why are children starving?

This passage has part of the answer – God loves righteousness and justice but we humans are not always righteous or just or loving. Scientists tell us that there is always enough food in the world to feed everyone but, sadly, we who have plenty do not often consider those who do not.

To think about:
How can we show God's unfailing love, His righteousness and His justice to those who are suffering?

Unfailing love

*H*ow precious is your unfailing love, O God! All humanity finds shelter in the shadow of your wings. You feed them from the abundance of your own house, letting them drink from your river of delights. For you are the fountain of life, the light by which we see. Pour out your unfailing love on those who love you; give justice to those with honest hearts.
Psalm 36:7–10 (NLT)

The psalmist proclaims that God's love is unfailing and his earnest prayer is that God will pour out His love on all who love Him. This follows the theme that all humanity can know God's provision, His love and His protection. God is the Giver of life and He is the light by which we can see and understand His ways. God longs that all people will know His unfailing love and so we, like the psalmist, have a responsibility to pray for those who do not yet know Him.

Pray for those who have plenty and do not feel the need for God's love.

Pray for those in countries where they have not heard of God's love.

Pray for the suffering who long for God's loving provision.

Prayer:
Loving God, please give me understanding to know how to pray for those who do not yet know Your unfailing love. Amen.

His love stands firm

I will sing of the LORD's great love for ever;
with my mouth I will make your faithfulness
known through all generations. I will declare that
your love stands firm for ever, that you established your
faithfulness in heaven itself. *Psalm 89:1–2*

This psalmist had no doubt whatever about God's love.
Can you say with him, 'I will declare that Your love
stands firm for ever ...'? As we grow older and look back
over our lives we can often see where God has guided,
provided, kept us safe, comforted and strengthened us.
Perhaps we didn't see it at the time, when circumstances
were difficult, but now we can testify that all through the
years His love for us has stood firm. What a privilege to
be able to tell our families, the younger generation, as
well as our friends, of God's faithfulness.

**Think about how you can tell about God's
great love:**
'Tell out, my soul, the glories of his word!
Firm is his promise, and his mercy sure.
Tell out, my soul, the greatness of the Lord
To children's children and for evermore!'
Timothy Dudley-Smith (1926-)
Printed by permission. See copyright page.

God's love is constant

*I*n the land of Uz there lived a man whose name was Job. This man was blameless and upright; he feared God and shunned evil. *Job 1:1*

Job was a good man. Nevertheless God tested him by allowing all sorts of calamities to come upon him. He lost his livestock, his servants and his family, and then was struck by a horrible illness, but he didn't lose his faith. He said to his friends: 'Keep silent and let me speak; then let come to me what may ... Though he slay me, yet will I hope in him.' *Job 13:13–15*

Job had much to learn about God – and although he wasn't always right, yet his faith remained firm throughout the hard times. And God's love for Job remained constant and when Job humbled himself, God rewarded him with health and prosperity again.

After Job had prayed for his friends, the LORD made him prosperous again and gave him twice as much as he had before. All his brothers and sisters and everyone who had known him before came and ate with him in his house. They comforted and consoled him over all the trouble the LORD had brought upon him ... The LORD blessed the latter part of Job's life more than the first. *Job 42:10–12*

Prayer:
Please help me to remember, Lord, when times are hard, that Your love for me is constant. Amen.

Sacrificial love

*T*he chief priests, the teachers of the law and the elders mocked him [Jesus]. 'He saved others,' they said, 'but he can't save himself! He's the King of Israel! Let him come down now from the cross, and we will believe in him. He trusts in God. Let God rescue him now if he wants him, for he said, "I am the Son of God."' In the same way the robbers who were crucified with him also heaped insults on him. From the sixth hour until the ninth hour darkness came over all the land. About the ninth hour Jesus cried out in a loud voice, *'Eloi, Eloi, lama sabachthani?'* – which means, 'My God, my God, why have you forsaken me?' *Matthew 27:41–46*

Even Jesus, on the cross, felt that His Father God had forsaken Him. We cannot know what it was like for Jesus to bear the sins of the whole world and to suffer intolerable pain and insults as He was dying that day, but the feeling that His beloved Father had forsaken Him must have been the worst part of all.

We know the end of the story though. God the Father had not forsaken Jesus; He rose again from death. Love triumphed and that love, God's love for you and me, remains constant forever.

Prayer:
Thank You, Father, that You did not forsake Your Son and You will never forsake me. Amen.

Using your gifts

There are different kinds of gifts, but the same Spirit. There are different kinds of service, but the same Lord. There are different kinds of working, but the same God works all of them in all men.
1 Corinthians 12:4–6

Each one should use whatever gift he has received to serve others, faithfully administering God's grace in its various forms. If anyone speaks, he should do it as one speaking the very words of God. If anyone serves, he should do it with the strength God provides, so that in all things God may be praised through Jesus Christ. To him be the glory and the power for ever and ever. Amen.
1 Peter 4:10–11

We all have different gifts and talents. Some we are born with, some we acquire as we go through life. Some are obvious and may lead to fame and fortune but for most of us our special gifts may seem very ordinary. It can be frustrating as we grow older not to be able to use the talents we had when we were younger – fingers may become too stiff to play the piano or knit. We may not be so active but, on the other hand, we have more leisure to develop gifts we didn't have time for before.

Prayer:
Thank You, Lord, for the gifts and talents You give me. Please show me how to use them in Your service now. Amen.

The gift of helping

*J*n Joppa there was a disciple named Tabitha ... who was always doing good and helping the poor. About that time she became sick and died ... so when the disciples heard that Peter was in Lydda, they sent two men to him and urged him, 'Please come at once!'

Peter went with them, and when he arrived he was taken upstairs to the room. All the widows stood around him, crying and showing him the robes and other clothing that Dorcas [Tabitha] had made while she was still with them. *Acts 9:36–39*

As this story goes on we learn that Peter prayed and brought Tabitha (who was also called Dorcas) back to life again so she could continue her work among the poor.

Tabitha had a practical gift – she could sew – and she used this gift to full advantage to help those who needed clothes. We are not all great preachers or evangelists but we can be just as useful in God's kingdom by using the practical gifts He gives us. Tabitha had a willing heart, she had compassion for the poor, she worked hard and she used her skill with sewing to help those in need.

Prayer:
Dear Lord, I am willing to use those gifts and skills that You have given me to help others. Please show me how. Amen.

The gift of craftsmanship

*T*hen the LORD said to Moses, 'See I have chosen Bezalel son of Uri, the son of Hur, of the tribe of Judah, and I have filled him with the Spirit of God, with skill, ability and knowledge in all kinds of crafts – to make artistic designs for work in gold, silver and bronze, to cut and set stones, to work in wood, and to engage in all kinds of craftsmanship ... Also I have given skill to all the craftsmen to make everything I have commanded you. *Exodus 31:1–6*

This story is about the construction of the tabernacle in the wilderness after the Children of Israel had escaped from Egypt. God had a definite plan for the tabernacle which He revealed to Moses and it was God who provided the skill needed to carry out those plans. The passage we have read makes it clear that it is God who gives special skills to people for the special tasks He wants them to do. He anointed Bezalel and the other craftsmen with His Holy Spirit and with artistic talents.

No doubt they also had to practise and hone those skills but they were then able and willing to do the work to which God had called them.

To think about:
What special skills do you have? They may be small or great but are you willing to use them in God's service?

The gift of understanding

*T*hen the king ... ordered Ashpenaz ... to bring in some of the Israelites from the royal family and the nobility ... Among these were ... Daniel, Hananiah, Mishael and Azariah ... To these four young men God gave knowledge and understanding of all kinds of literature and learning. And Daniel could understand visions and dreams of all kinds. *Daniel 1:3,6,17*

These are the numbers of the men armed for battle who came to David at Hebron to turn Saul's kingdom over to him, as the LORD had said ... men of Issachar, who understood the times and knew what Israel should do ... *1 Chronicles 12:23,32*

These two short stories happened hundreds of years apart yet serve to illustrate the need, in all times and in all situations, for men and women of understanding. This also is a God-given gift – the ability to assess a situation, to understand the implications and know what to do about it. It also takes practice and experience. The world today is very different from the world we knew in our youth when, despite two world wars, there was more stability, belief in God and righteousness in financial dealings. As older people we can use our understanding to help the younger generation.

Prayer:
Please help me, Lord, to use wisely the understanding You give me. Amen.

The gift of hospitality

After this, Paul left Athens and went to Corinth. There he met a Jew named Aquila, a native of Pontus, who had recently come from Italy with his wife Priscilla, because Claudius had ordered all the Jews to leave Rome. Paul went to see them, and because he was a tentmaker as they were, he stayed and worked with them. ... [a Jew named Apollos] began to speak boldly in the synagogue. When Priscilla and Aquila heard him, they invited him to their home and explained the way of God more adequately. *Acts 18:1–3,26*

Greet Priscilla and Aquila ... Greet also the church that meets at their house. *Romans 16:3,5*

Aquila and Priscilla were a remarkable couple. Despite having had to uproot themselves from their home in Rome because of the Emperor Claudius' pogrom they were nevertheless ready to open their homes, first in Corinth and then in Ephesus, to fellow believers. They had the gift of hospitality.

Whatever our homes are like, large or small, whether we live in a mansion or just one room we can all be hospitable, welcoming our family, friends and neighbours and encouraging them in Jesus as Aquila and Priscilla did.

Prayer:
Thank You, Lord, for the gift of hospitality. Please help me to be welcoming to all those who come to visit me, whether invited or uninvited. Amen.

The gift of evangelism

*A*ndrew, Simon Peter's brother, was one of the two who heard what John had said and who had followed Jesus. The first thing Andrew did was to find his brother Simon and tell him, 'We have found the Messiah' (that is, the Christ). And he brought him to Jesus. *John 1:40-42*

As Jesus was getting into the boat, the man who had been demon-possessed begged to go with him. Jesus did not let him, but said, 'Go home to your family and tell them how much the Lord has done for you …' *Mark 5:18–19*

We are not all gifted to be great evangelists like St Paul or Billy Graham, speaking to thousands about God's gift of salvation, but ordinary people like you and me can still be useful in telling others about our faith. The first thing Andrew did when he met Jesus was to go and find his brother. He didn't want Simon to miss out on his exciting discovery. And the man who had been demon-possessed went home and told his family, then his neighbours, what Jesus had done for him and the news spread throughout the region.

We all have a responsibility to share our faith with those close to us and God will help us to know what to say.

Prayer:
Please, Lord Jesus, give me the courage and the words to share my faith with others. Amen.

Using our gifts

*J*ust as each of us has one body with many members, and these members do not all have the same function, so in Christ we who are many form one body, and each member belongs to all the others. We have different gifts, according to the grace given us. If a man's gift is prophesying, let him use it in proportion to his faith. If it is serving, let him serve; if it is teaching, let him teach; if it is encouraging, let him encourage; if it is contributing to the needs of others, let him give generously; if it is leadership, let him govern diligently; if it is showing mercy, let him do it cheerfully.
Romans 12:4–8

We have seen over the past week that we all have different gifts. No gift is more important than any other. You may have a great preacher in your church – but how could he function if there was no one to clean the church or make the coffee? Missionaries could not do their work without the generous giving of finance. Your neighbours might never hear of the saving grace of Christ if you do not tell them.

And above all, we can use the gift of prayer to uphold our fellow workers in Christ's kingdom.

Prayer:
Please show me, Lord, what gifts You have given me and help me to use them faithfully and diligently in Your service. Amen.

Commended by Jesus

She gave her all

*A*s he looked up, Jesus saw the rich putting their gifts into the temple treasury. He also saw a poor widow put in two very small copper coins. 'I tell you the truth,' he said, 'this poor widow has put in more than all the others. All these people gave their gifts out of their wealth; but she out of her poverty put in all she had to live on.' *Luke 21:1–4*

This widow would have been in the part of the Temple known as the Court of Women, where there were thirteen funnel-shaped containers for receiving the Temple tax and free-will offerings. The rich would throw their money in ostentatiously, hoping others would see how generous they were, but we can imagine the poor woman being ashamed of how little she had to give and creeping up quietly to put in her small offering.

Jesus saw, however, and knowing that she had given all she had, commended her in front of the crowds. We may feel that we have little to give to God, whether it be our money, our talents or our time, but that doesn't matter – if we just give ourselves, all that we have and are, He is pleased with us.

Prayer:
Dear God, I give myself afresh to You today; please take all that I have and am and use me in Your service. Amen.

He said, 'Thank You'

*A*s [Jesus] was going into a village, ten men who had leprosy met him. They stood at a distance and called out in a loud voice, 'Jesus, Master, have pity on us!' When he saw them, he said, 'Go, show yourselves to the priests.' And as they went they were cleansed. One of them, when he saw he was healed, came back, praising God in a loud voice. He threw himself at Jesus' feet and thanked him – and he was a Samaritan.

Jesus asked, 'Were not all ten cleansed? Where are the other nine?' *Luke 17:12–17*

In Bible times those with leprosy were not allowed to associate with other people, so these ten men quite rightly did not approach Jesus but shouted to Him from a distance.

Jesus took pity on them and all ten were cleansed from their disease. Only one, however, came back to thank Him, and this time he had the courage to go right up to Jesus and throw himself down at His feet in gratitude.

There is something about saying 'thank you' that brings us closer to God and to those who help us day by day. Jesus was pleased with the man who came back to say, 'Thank You!'

Prayer:
Dear Lord Jesus, thank You for all that You have done for me throughout my life and are still doing today. Amen.

She showed her love to Jesus

*W*hile [Jesus] was in Bethany ... a woman came with an alabaster jar of very expensive perfume, made of pure nard. She broke the jar and poured the perfume on his head.

Some of those present were saying indignantly to one another, 'Why this waste of perfume? It could have been sold for more than a year's wages and the money given to the poor.' And they rebuked her harshly.

'Leave her alone,' said Jesus. 'Why are you bothering her? She has done a beautiful thing to me.' *Mark 14:3–6*

Whatever we do for other people we are doing for Jesus. Helping the poor, or anyone who needs our help in any way, is part of our service to Him. But Jesus commended this woman for ministering to Him alone – showing her love for Him by pouring the very expensive perfume on His head. To some it looked like a waste of money.

Likewise, to some in our generation going to church to worship God might look like a waste of time. Praying when we could have been doing something practical might seem a waste of time. But showing our love to God Himself is never a waste of time.

Prayer:
Dear Lord Jesus, I want to pour my love out to You as the woman poured her perfume. Lord, I love You, I worship and adore You. Amen.

He had faith

*A*s Jesus and his disciples, together with a large crowd, were leaving the city, a blind man, Bartimaeus ... was sitting by the roadside begging. When he heard that it was Jesus of Nazareth, he began to shout, 'Jesus, Son of David, have mercy on me!' Many rebuked him and told him to be quiet, but he shouted all the more, 'Son of David, have mercy on me!' Jesus stopped and said, 'Call him.' So they called to the blind man, 'Cheer up! On your feet! He's calling you.' Throwing his cloak aside he jumped to his feet and came to Jesus. 'What do you want me to do for you?' Jesus asked him. The blind man said, 'Rabbi, I want to see.' 'Go,' said Jesus, 'your faith has healed you.' Immediately he received his sight and followed Jesus along the road.
Mark 10:46–52

Bartimaeus had not been able to see the miracles Jesus performed but he believed what he had heard. By persevering in his loud cries he showed that he believed that Jesus would help even a blind beggar. In some ways we are like Bartimaeus; we have not seen Jesus perform miracles but we have heard about them and read about them in the Bible. So we, too, can have faith that Jesus will perform miracles for us.

Prayer:
Lord Jesus, I believe You can still perform miracles today. Amen.

The faith of a foreigner

*W*hen Jesus had entered Capernaum, a centurion came to him, asking for help. 'Lord,' he said, 'my servant lies at home paralysed and in terrible suffering.' Jesus said to him, 'I will go and heal him.'

The centurion said, 'Lord, I do not deserve to have you come under my roof. But just say the word, and my servant will be healed ...' When Jesus heard this, he was astonished and said to those following him, 'I tell you the truth, I have not found anyone in Israel with such great faith ...' Then Jesus said to the centurion, 'Go! It will be done just as you believed it would.' And his servant was healed at that very hour. *Matthew 8:5–13*

The centurion was Roman, not Jewish. He did not have the background knowledge of the Jewish Scriptures or the prophecies concerning the coming Messiah yet he had heard about the miracles of healing that Jesus was performing and he recognised His authority. That recognition enabled him to believe that Jesus could just say the word from a distance and the servant would be healed.

Jesus commended him for his faith. We, too, have heard of Jesus' miracles, so we, too, can have faith in Him.

Prayer:
Dear Lord Jesus, please help me to believe. Help me, like the centurion, to have faith that You can do anything I ask. Amen.

He was humble

*J*esus told this parable, 'Two men went up to the temple to pray, one a Pharisee and the other a tax collector. The Pharisee stood up and prayed about himself: "God, I thank you that I am not like other men – robbers, evildoers, adulterers – or even like this tax collector. I fast twice a week and give a tenth of all I get." But the tax collector stood at a distance. He would not even look up to heaven, but beat his breast and said, "God have mercy on me, a sinner." I tell you that this man, rather than the other, went home justified before God.' *Luke 18:9–14*

Jesus told this story to people who thought they were better than everyone else.

Two very different attitudes to prayer – the Pharisee prayed with pride to show everyone how good he was. That doesn't cut any ice with God, who knows our hearts as well as our deeds. However good we are we can never measure up to the perfect standard that Jesus Himself set for us.

The tax collector prayed with humility, recognising that he was a sinner who needed God's forgiveness and mercy. His was the sort of prayer that Jesus commended.

Prayer:
I, too, Lord Jesus, recognise that I am a sinner and I thank You that You gave Your life for me so that I may be forgiven. Amen.

Mary chose the better place

*J*esus ... came to a village where a woman named Martha opened her home to him. She had a sister called Mary, who sat at the Lord's feet listening to what he said. But Martha was distracted by all the preparations that had to be made. She came to him and asked, 'Lord, don't you care that my sister has left me to do all the work by myself? Tell her to help me!'

'Martha, Martha,' the Lord answered, 'you are worried and upset about many things, but only one thing is needed. Mary has chosen what is better, and it will not be taken away from her.' *Luke 10:38–42*

Mary was not being lazy, she wanted to take advantage of Jesus' presence in their home and listen to all He had to say. She knew what was important about His visit whereas Martha was so anxious about preparing a meal that she didn't have time to sit with the guests. Jesus was right – a simple meal would have sufficed and would have given Martha time to come out of the kitchen and enjoy the company.

Are you like Martha or like Mary? So busy that you don't have time to sit and pray, enjoying God's presence? Or, as Mary did, taking time with God first?

Prayer:
Please help me, Lord, to be calm and take time in Your presence every day. Amen.

God, my refuge

*I*n you, O LORD, I have taken refuge;
    let me never be put to shame;
  deliver me in your righteousness.
Turn your ear to me,
  come quickly to my rescue;
be my rock of refuge,
  a strong fortress to save me.
Since you are my rock and my fortress,
    for the sake of your name lead me and guide me.
Psalm 31:1–3

This is a wonderful prayer! The psalmist places his complete trust in God, recognising that He is a safe refuge in any circumstance. God is likened to a rock, a firm, stable place to stand on or a shield to hide behind. And a fortress – a place to run into and know protection and provision. In this world and in our individual lives there are sometimes difficulties we don't know how to handle. It could be illness or family troubles, financial worries or bereavement – times when we need direction and don't know what to do. Always we can put our trust in God, who is strong and able.

To do:
Read through these verses again, think about the words and use them as a prayer, for yourself.

I will praise You

I will exalt you, my God the King;
    I will praise your name for ever and ever.
Every day I will praise you
and extol your name for ever and ever.
Great is the LORD and most worthy of praise;
   his greatness no-one can fathom.
One generation will commend your works to another;
   they will tell of your mighty acts. *Psalm 145:1–4*

'Every day I will praise you …' the psalmist declares.
Not when he feels like it, or when the sun is shining and
everything is going well. Not 'maybe' or 'I might' but
'I will'. It is a declaration of intention but also a promise
to the Lord that each day he will spend time praising our
great God who is so worthy of our praise and adoration.
I wonder if you and I can say the same?

When we wake up each morning God is there –
what a good time to start praising Him! Praise Him for
His love, the beauty of His creation, His power, His
compassion and His grace – the list is endless!

Prayer:
Lord God, I *will* praise You morning, noon and
night, because You are worthy of my praise all the
time. Amen.